FINDING FULFILLMENT WITHIN

A TRANSFORMATIONAL JOURNEY TO HAPPINESS, PEACE, AND JOY

JULIE RIZZO

PRAISES FOR FINDING FULFILLMENT WITHIN

If we were rating this book—I give it 5 plus stars! *Finding Fulfillment Within* captivated me with the author's own personal journey of seeking joy and happiness. It will make you laugh, cry, see yourself in her and want to keep turning the page to delve more into her thoughts and lessons as you learn things to help you overcome your own obstacles in life. A captivating and motivational read that not only tells the author's story, she shows you how and gives you the tools and lessons to transform your life to finding your own personal joy and balance to tapping into areas you didn't even know existed. *Finding Fulfilllment Within* is truly a lesson in life, personal joy, and finding your own fulfillment, a must read for anyone ready to embark on and change their existence and live their best life.
~ Jenn

Finding Fulfillment Within is a powerful journey to becoming happier, healthier, and more peaceful. Julie Rizzo takes us through her own powerful story of discovering her life needed to change for her to live her fullest life. Her emphasis on nutrition and how it ties to overall health take the process of life improvement full circle. Her workbook allowed me to reflect and plan changes in my own life. This book is a must read!
~ Colleen

I found *Finding Fulfillment Within* to be very relatable, inspiring, and uplifting! As I began to read this book, I realized that I could relate to most of the challenges she was facing and that my life was not set in stone. It was inspiring to see how she took the mind, body, and soul approach to making real change in her life. She shows you it is easier to stay positive and on track by setting smaller, more attainable goals with your ultimate goal in mind. I have benefited from this book personally and professionally. I have a large team that I work with and believe this book is a must read for them!
~ Kirk

Julie Rizzo's book *Finding Fulfillment Within* has been very empowering. It has helped me to take the necessary steps to change the negative behavior that has been impacting my life. I have put into place what I have learned in her book by setting goals for healthier eating habits replacing processed foods with more natural whole foods. I have also started a diary to determine how different foods impact my health and to try to eliminate stress eating. She has taught me that we need to slow down, relax, and savor the journey. The more we work on transitioning from the negative to the positive and learn to be fulfilled the happier we will be.

~ Kim

The first line went straight to the point and I was hooked! "Our thoughts, actions and behaviors all influence the life we choose to live— Choose Wisely!" This book is a clear, concise guide to help us uncover the negative and unhealthy choices we have ingrained into our lives and habits. Then sensible steps toward eliminating what doesn't work and moving toward a life filled with happiness, peace, and joy!

~ Julie

As a working mother of two I have struggled at times trying to juggle my personal and professional life, always putting myself last. Julie's vulnerability makes this book relatable. Her frequent reminders to forgive yourself and to not expect perfection make this book comforting rather than other "self-help" books which are only stress provoking. As a medical professional I appreciate that it can be difficult to explain to others the complexities of nutrition and how it affects our health. Julie lays out the basics in a simple format which is understandable for the reader. *Finding Fulfillment Within* is an easy, non-complicated read which has a little something for everyone.

~ Candace

After reading *Finding Fulfillment Within*, I kept fighting back the feeling that my life would have been so different had I read this book 20 years ago. This book gives you the tools to make real, positive changes in your life and find inner peace. I feel confident that my future self will be able to continue to apply all the useful tools Julie provides in order to stay on a path of true self-improvement!
~ Rhonda

Finding Fulfillment Within is a brief but inspiring guide to help you rediscover your happiness. The author invites readers to take control of their health in all aspects - mental, physical, and emotional, and walks readers through different exercises to retain this control. This book truly helps one rediscover their life's purpose and finding their fulfillment from within.
~ Rachel

So, I have to admit, I am not a big book reader. It's not that I don't enjoy it—I just never give myself time to actually sit down and allow it. But when I read *Finding Fulfilment Within*, I felt as if I was looking into a mirror reflecting back on my life. Reading this book has provided me with the courage to start taking care of myself. Anyone that finds themselves always taking care of everyone else (which a majority of us do) will find this book as a fresh start to be the very best you can be for YOURSELF! I loved the way it is broken down into sections: nurturing our mindset, how to fuel your body, and enhancing our spirit. This book is a must read for anyone who is ready to take control over their own destiny and truly find HAPPINESS within!
~ Cindy

For my mom. Although you aren't here to read it, I believe you were with me as I wrote it. Together we will help others find their happiness, peace, and joy. I love you and I miss you!

TABLE OF CONTENTS

THOUGHTS, ACTIONS, AND BEHAVIORS— WHAT NEEDS TO CHANGE?

Our thoughts, actions, and behaviors all influence the life we choose to live. Choose wisely. ~ Julie Rizzo

Negative self-talk was one of the biggest obstacles throughout my life. Looking at everything wrong, instead of everything right, had become a habit. My thoughts were almost always negative. You can't be happy when your thoughts are full of negativity. I am here to tell you: it's impossible. Once I identified this unhealthy, destructive behavior, I realized it was preventing me from living in happiness, with peace and joy. I made the conscious decision to dig down deep and discover what needed to change, so I would not continue to live in unhappiness.

Many times, I would say jokingly, "You know what? It must be me! Everyone around me is good. I am the one that has the problem." As I thought about this on a deeper level, I realized that statement could not have been any closer to the truth. It was me. I was critical of everyone and everything in my life. I didn't take responsibility for any of it, because I didn't believe I was part of the problem. The harsher truth? I was most of the problem.

As you can imagine, this was not an easy thing to accept. I asked myself, How long have I done this? Why did I do this? Can I change it? As I began this journey to find fulfillment with happiness, peace, and joy, I explored my past behaviors to see how I arrived at this place of unhappiness.

For years, most everything I did was to please others—parents, teachers, friends, co-workers, and bosses. Getting good grades was driven by a deep need to please my parents and teachers. I said "yes" to friends who asked me to go out when I wanted to sit on the couch and read a book. Instead of saying "no," I found myself at a bar late at night because I didn't want to disappoint my friends. Working 12-hour days as a salaried employee, plus weekends to "get the job done," was all to prove to my boss I could do what it took to succeed. I found myself frustrated when others were out enjoying themselves while I was still working.

As if my willingness to put everyone else's happiness first wasn't enough, I had to be perfect at everything I did. Again, not for myself, but for everyone else. Getting 90% for the A wasn't enough; it had to be 100%. Saying "yes" to my friend wasn't enough; I offered to drive and pay the tab, too. Putting in long hours at work wasn't enough; I had to make sure everything I did was perfect. Nothing mattered except making others happy, even at the expense of my happiness.

Fear invaded, and my life grew more and more debilitating. It was pervasive. I was afraid of not giving or being enough. I was afraid of disappointing people. I was afraid of change, failure, and saying the wrong thing. I was afraid of what people thought of me, of not being accepted. Afraid of the unknown.

Getting too wrapped up in fear causes turmoil and unhappiness in your life. Fear creates a fight-or-flight response, leaving you with a feeling of insurmountable anxiety. When uncontrolled, fear can lead to overwhelm and depression.

It took me a long time to get here, but I can say that I am finally finding happiness and discovering peace and joy. While some habits were hard to unlearn, taking the first step was the best gift I could give myself. I believe I will always be on this journey, each day bringing further clarity and understanding. Choosing to put myself at the top of my list has shown me that I am enough, just as I am. So far, this has been the most significant discovery in my journey, and it has made a profound difference in the way I live my life. Every day I am one step closer to happiness and I remain fulfilled with peace and joy.

In this book, I will take you on my journey to wellness and share honestly what I have learned. Although you may already know some of these lessons, you might have been unable to activate them. Perhaps you believe it will be too hard, don't know where to start, or feel stuck. Mindset and habit change begin this journey. I will show you how to nurture your mind, body, and spirit. I will guide you through this journey. This book will help you set goals and put accountability into place to achieve them. The hardest part will be stepping out of your comfort zone and moving forward from planning to doing. But I have faith in the process and in you. These steps worked for me, and I believe they can work for you, too.

Are you ready to begin your journey to fulfillment and find your happiness, peace, and joy? There are workbook sections throughout this book which will provide you opportunities to reflect. The entire workbook is available to download at https://findingfulfillmentwithin.com/workbook.html. This was designed as a guide to help you uncover the behaviors and habits you want to change along your journey.

I will ask some insightful questions throughout the book, and ask you to put in writing your thoughts as they are in the moment. As you continue setting goals and tracking outcomes, you will evaluate where you started, compared to where you find yourself throughout your journey. By doing this you will be able to see the progress you are making. Get ready to embark on a journey that will undoubtedly change your life and lead you to find your happiness, peace, and joy.

1

NURTURING OUR MINDS

1

MINDSET— ACCEPTING HABIT CHANGE

"A change in bad habits leads to a change in life." ~ Jenny Craig

Think about this as we get started. All habits, good or bad, are a choice. We choose our thoughts and actions. We decide what ideas we allow in our minds, how we react to situations, and the words we speak. Your habits define the person you will become. Improvement can be as simple as looking at your patterns and replacing negative practices with positive ones.

What habits are you looking to change? As you begin this journey, you will examine the way you think. Once you recognize how your thoughts impact your life, other changes will seem within reach.

How do you talk to yourselves? Would you speak to a friend that way? The answer to that question for me was no. I didn't give myself the grace and love I naturally gave others. To change that, I first identified when I began down the path of negative self-talk, and then made a conscious decision to move towards positivity.

What habits do you need to change to achieve positive self-talk? What triggers cause you to go down a negative path? Let's identify those triggers, look at your current responses, and see what changes you can make to choose healthier ones. Grab that workbook, or write your response in the space provided, and let's start on your journey.

SITUATION & RESPONSE:

It will be a busy day at work: back-to-back meetings, projects due, and deadlines to meet. Write down your thoughts.

_____
_____
_____
_____
_____
_____

Look at your response above. Is there a more positive way to think? What does that look like? What habits need to shift? Write down your thoughts.

_____
_____
_____
_____
_____
_____

Full workbook is available for download at:
https://findingfulfillmentwithin.com/workbook.html

1

Overwhelmed. Overworked. Unfair. Unrealistic. A different job would be easier. I won't be able to get everything done. I can't wait for a day off.

Is this where your thoughts took you? How do you feel right now? Frustrated, angry, exhausted?

If these were your first thoughts, you are not alone. Most of my days began this way, and these are the same responses many people have given me when asked this question. The thoughts we allow to consume us determine our outlook. It is essential to recognize this and make a conscious decision to guard what you allow into your mind.

Is a negative mindset a trigger for you? What would happen if you identified the negative mindset and moved toward a positive one? What does that look like for you? The happiness of your life depends on the quality of what you think. If your thoughts are consistently negative, you can't expect to live a happy life with peace and joy.

What if the first thoughts in your mind were these instead:

I've set my schedule, and it is going to be a busy day, but I've put together a plan that will allow me to accomplish great things. Everything I achieve today will bring me closer to completing the projects that are due and the deadlines that I need to meet. Although I may not finish everything today, all my hard work will bring me closer to reaching my final desired outcome. I will show up today, give it my all, and end this day with a great sense of accomplishment.

How do you feel now? Positive, organized, energized, focused, happy, accomplished? Are you ready to step into the day with a positive mindset and achieve great things? Do you see the difference? Think about this: you changed your outlook for the day just by changing your thoughts. This is one example of how negative self-talk prevents us from being happy. Once we identify this, we can choose the positive direction.

Think about where you live. You plan to go to the mall to buy a gift. How many different routes can you take to get there? At least two, right? You take the one that leads you to the mall the quickest, with the least amount of lights, traffic, and construction. You will choose the best possible route. This should be the same direction we take in our lives, the best possible route leading us to our destination. You will arrive with as little obstacles and negativity as possible, giving you a sense of fulfillment with peace, happiness, and joy when you get there.

Roadblocks and setbacks will be part of this journey, even with the best intentions. Running into these obstacles does not indicate failure. We are imperfect humans, born with feelings and emotions. Difficult days are going to happen. When they do, identify what prevented the day from being great and move past it, without falling back into bad habits. Finding yourself better today than you were yesterday is a significant accomplishment on this journey.

Evaluate where you are each week. It is crucial to track progress and identify where you've made changes in your thinking. Be sure to give yourself praise as you evaluate your week. Have self-gratitude as you take steps to reach your goals. We will cover setting goals and tracking outcomes near the end of this book.

Remember, this is your journey to find fulfillment within yourself and live your life with happiness, peace, and joy. Each small step propels you forward toward achieving this.

"Your mind is a sacred enclosure into which nothing harmful can enter except by your permission."
~ Arnold Bennett

2

SELF FIRST,
OTHERS SECOND

*"Putting yourself first is not selfish.
Quite the opposite. You must put your
happiness and health first before you can
be of help to anyone else." ~ Simon Sinek*

How often have you found yourself doing things to make others happy, only to realize it caused you unhappiness? "Put your oxygen mask on first before assisting others." Do you recall these instructions that are given on planes before takeoff? Only once we have taken care of ourselves can we begin to take care of others. Self-care was difficult for me.

Have you been in a situation where someone asks you to do something, and you immediately say "yes," even though it isn't something you want to do? When you say "yes," are you thinking of a way to back out gracefully? Why do we react like this? Is it a desire to be accepted and pleasing? Or fear of disappointing and not belonging?

SITUATION & RESPONSE:

A group from work invites you to attend an event Friday evening. You were looking forward to going home and relaxing. Write down your thoughts.

_____

_____

_____

_____

_____

_____

Look at your response above. Is there a more positive way to think? What does that look like? What habits need to shift? Write down your thoughts.

_____

_____

_____

_____

_____

_____

Full workbook is available for download at:
https://findingfulfillmentwithin.com/workbook.html

I don't want to go. I was looking forward to going home and relaxing. If I don't go, they will think poorly of me. They will talk about me if I'm not there. They will think I don't want to be a part of the group. I won't get invited again if I don't go this time. I need to just suck it up and go. Did any of these thoughts make your list, as they used to mine?

You are who you are. Most people will like you for you, but you will never be able to please everyone. That is unrealistic and unattainable. Be a good person, and do what brings you happiness. Worrying about what others think of you doesn't change their way of thinking. Everyone is entitled to their own opinions. Sometimes they will be identical to yours, sometimes they will be different, and that is okay.

Know your priorities. This will guide you in knowing when you can say "yes" to others and will make it clear when to say "no." Immediately committing is not a requirement you need to meet. It is okay to say, "Let me think about it, and I will let you know." Allow yourself time to evaluate if it is truly something you want to commit to.

There are two questions we need to ask ourselves in any situation: Is doing this going to bring me happiness, peace, or joy? And, is this something I want to do? If the answers to these questions are "no," you have the choice to decline. No further explanation is needed. Simply say, "I appreciate you inviting me, but I am not going to be able to make it this time."

If your final decision is to say "yes," say it without setting expectations or hoping for something in return. I had a bad habit of doing this, and it ultimately led to disappointment and resentment. Don't set yourself up to be disappointed because you create a picture in your mind that isn't necessarily going to happen.

Meet your needs first before you step up to meet the needs of others. We hope and expect others to do extraordinary things for us, but we are quite capable of doing these ourselves. Don't wait for others to make you happy; make yourself happy! Buy the flowers, light the candles, and spend quiet time alone. Permit yourself to do the things that bring happiness into your life.

3 YOU DON'T HAVE TO BE PERFECT

1

"Perfectionism doesn't make you feel perfect; it makes you feel inadequate." ~ Maria Shriver

I know I am not alone when it comes to believing that perfection was the only acceptable outcome. I spent my life searching for perfection because I thought I needed to be perfect in everything I did. I realized that perfection is unattainable. Living my life this way created an unnecessary expectation and burden. When you seek perfection, you see what was not accomplished and miss seeing all that was. Stop striving for perfection. Do your best and learn from the mistakes you make along the way.

SITUATION & RESPONSE:

You are hosting a get-together at your home. Everyone is bringing a side dish, and you are providing the main course. Before everyone arrives, you check on the main course in the oven, and it is burnt. Write down your thoughts.

_____
_____
_____
_____
_____
_____

Look at your response above. Is there a more positive way to think? What does that look like? What habits need to shift? Write down your thoughts.

_____
_____
_____
_____
_____
_____

Full workbook is available for download at:
https://findingfulfillmentwithin.com/workbook.html

1

Dinner is ruined. Everyone will be upset. I will be embarrassed. This is horrible. What was I thinking when I planned this dinner?

Were any of these your thoughts? How much energy have you spent trying to be perfect? Do you feel an overwhelming sense of failure when you are not perfect? Do you think people will think less of you if you make a mistake? It isn't important what other people think. When I learned to let go of trying to be perfect in everything I did, I had a better attitude and a lot less stress. Learn to look at what went right instead of what went wrong.

Instead of the negative thoughts, what if your thoughts were more like this?

We are going to have a good laugh about this! The real reason we are together is to enjoy each other's company. We can always order something out. This isn't the end of the world. Next time, I will make this easier on myself. At least we have a lot of wine. Are you smiling and feeling less stressed and anxious now?

I love to paint, so I bought several wall hangings for our outside area that required painting. I painted three of the pieces but was so critical of my painting, I stopped. There was always an imperfection or something I could have done better.

After seven years, I came across them in a box in the garage. Three that I had painted along with all the others I didn't. I pulled them out and finished painting them. I realized my best was good enough. They aren't perfect, but I enjoyed every minute I spent painting them. I stopped focusing on the imperfections and enjoyed the pleasure I felt when I painted and hung them up. I sincerely love each one of them. Doing your best should always be good enough. You don't have to be perfect. Don't let perfectionism ruin your joy.

"Strive for continuous improvement, instead of perfection." ~ *Kim Collins*

4

FORGIVENESS OF OTHERS AND OURSELVES

"We must develop and maintain the capacity to forgive. He who is devoid of power to forgive is devoid of the power to love." ~ Martin Luther King Jr.

Forgiveness of others, as well as ourselves, can be extremely challenging. When someone hurts you deeply, the emotions related to that hurt are devastating. Holding on to hurt and anger without freely forgiving impacts our own happiness. When we don't forgive, anger and resentment grow. When we allow these feelings to consume us, in the end, the person we hurt the most is ourself.

SITUATION & RESPONSE:

Your spouse or significant other does something hurtful to you in your relationship. Write down your thoughts.

_____
_____
_____
_____
_____
_____

Look at your response above. Is there a more positive way to think? What does that look like? What habits need to shift? Write down your thoughts.

_____
_____
_____
_____
_____
_____

Full workbook is available for download at:
https://findingfulfillmentwithin.com/workbook.html

I can't believe they did that to me. How could they do that? They knew how much that was going to hurt me. They certainly didn't think about me before they did that. I am so upset. They are going to pay for what they did. I am never going to get past this. There is no way they care about me. What will others think when they find out what happened?

How long do you hold onto these thoughts and feelings? Hours, days, weeks, possibly months or even years? As you hold onto this hurt and anger, how happy are you? You may have moved past it temporarily, but if you don't sincerely forgive, when you think of it again, you will feel the same hurt and anger you did when it happened.

What if you replaced hurt with compassion? How does this look?

I know they care about me. They didn't realize how bad it would hurt me. They have had a bad day. They are hurting or fearful and don't know how else to deal with it. I will not let this situation replay itself in my mind. I will forgive and release the hurt and anger. I will not continue to hold onto it.

Learning to forgive others whole-heartedly releases this anger and resentment. It frees us to live in happiness, peace, and joy. Forgiveness does not mean we are condoning others' actions or pretending the situation never happened. It also does not mean we are allowing other people to take advantage of us. Forgiveness is not letting others' actions harm our life or the way we choose to live it.

Do you choose to move forward with forgiveness, or do you decide to hold onto anger and resentment? We have the choice to move forward with or without that person in our life. We are not obligated to reconcile with someone who has hurt us. But we can't move forward in peace without forgiving fully.

Choosing not to forgive ourselves can be as destructive to our happiness as not forgiving others. Sometimes forgiving ourselves is more complicated than forgiving others. We are usually willing to give others the benefit of the doubt, but not ourselves. Forgiving ourselves empowers us to let go of the past so that we can move forward knowing we did the best we could at the time. We can all pin-point situations from the past where we would make different choices if given the opportunity. However, you cannot change the past, so don't keep living in it.

We need to embrace the mistakes we have made and learn to forgive ourselves. By taking ownership and accountability for our mistakes, we can acknowledge and move past them. As we heard earlier, perfection is unattainable. We are all human, and mistakes will happen. Love yourself enough to forgive yourself as well as others.

"Forgiveness does not change the past, but it does enlarge the future."
~ Paul Lewis Boese

5

FAITH OR FEAR: YOUR CHOOSE

"Faith and fear both demand you believe in something you cannot see. You choose." ~ Bob Proctor

Fear consumed my life. There were so many times when fear prevented me from moving forward. This fear was debilitating. I can only compare it with a phone call in the middle of the night that causes the hair on the back of your neck to stand up. Living with daily fear had an adverse effect on my health and life.

I seldom found myself stepping out first in faith. Faith, for me, is having a deep sense of belief in something. Faith in ourselves tells us that we can accomplish anything we set out to do. When fear and doubt enter our thoughts, we can acknowledge these feelings and resist the urge to give in to them by moving forward in faith.

SITUATION & RESPONSE:

There is something you have been thinking about doing for a while. You see this often in your mind, but you haven't done it yet. Why? Write down your thoughts.

_____

_____

_____

_____

_____

_____

Look at your response above. Is there a more positive way to think? What does that look like? What habits need to shift? Write down your thoughts.

_____

_____

_____

_____

_____

_____

Full workbook is available for download at:
https://findingfulfillmentwithin.com/workbook.html

I am afraid of making a change. I'm comfortable where I am. It will be too much work. I doubt it can be accomplished. I will make mistakes. I fear the unknown outcome. I fear the possibility of success.

Don't let fear and doubt be obstacles. You only have one life to live. You can either take risks, or potentially lose the chance to reach your dreams. Each of our experiences teach us lessons. Are you willing to learn from those lessons instead of fearing them?

Let's choose to replace fear with faith. Say this once in your mind and then again out loud with conviction.

I believe in myself. I can do anything I choose to do. I have faith in myself. I am great. I am willing to put in the hard work needed to accomplish this. I will put doubt and fear aside, and I will move forward with faith and belief. Mistakes are lessons to learn from along the way. I will move forward without allowing fear or mistakes to get in my way. I choose to live my life in faith.

Step outside your comfort zone. Great things happen when we are uncomfortable. Look for those opportunities and step into them with faith. Believe in yourself. The thoughts in our minds are what prevent us from becoming great. When feelings of doubt show up, recognize them, and quickly replace them with belief.

We typically lean toward thinking the worst. Trust that when things don't go the way you want them to go; it is because something better is around the corner. Choose to think positively by choosing faith over fear. Calm and peace became more present in my life when I started choosing faith. I learned to put fear and doubt aside and stopped expecting the worst to happen. I have moved forward in my life with renewed purpose. You can do this too. The choice is yours to make.

6

LETTING WORRY GO AND CLAIMING PEACE OF MIND

"Worrying does not take away tomorrow's troubles. It takes away today's peace." ~ Unknown

How much time do we spend worrying about the past and future? My life was consumed with worry. Analyzing past situations and determining how I could have handled them better, worrying about the future with all the "what-ifs," planning for things that would never happen. I am here to tell you, worrying has never changed the outcome. I gave away many years of my happiness to worry.

I believed that if I tried to anticipate what could happen and thought through all the outcomes, I would be able to make any situation turn out the way I wanted. The worry this created was overwhelming. It negatively affected both my physical and mental health. I experienced anxiety and overwhelm in my life, and wasted so much time and energy worrying. I didn't let myself focus on the life I was presently living.

SITUATION & RESPONSE:

You are interviewing for a new job this week. How do you feel? Write down your thoughts.

_____
_____
_____
_____
_____
_____

Look at your response above. Is there a more positive way to think? What does that look like? What habits need to shift? Write down your thoughts.

_____
_____
_____
_____
_____
_____

Full workbook is available for download at:
https://findingfulfillmentwithin.com/workbook.html

I am nervous. I am doubtful of my qualifications. I am uncomfortable during interviews. I am fearful of not getting the job. What if I don't have the right answers?

What if your mind-set was confidence instead of doubt?

I am excited to have this interview. I know I am qualified for this position. I believe in myself and my abilities. I will show up with confidence. I am the candidate for this position.

The real power is knowing and accepting that if this doesn't work out, other opportunities will come your way. Ending worry starts with determining what you have control over and letting go of the rest. In some situations we have no power in deciding the outcome. Identify the things you worry about and stop repeating them in your mind. Write them down and voice them out loud.

Ask yourself these questions: *Is this a problem I can solve? Is there anything within my control that can help provide the outcome I am looking for? Is the worry I have a productive or an unproductive worry?* If you can do something to solve the problem right now, this is a productive worry. Instead of worrying, do something about it. You are in control. Unproductive worry is the opposite—it comes from the "what-ifs" in life that we worry about but have no control over.

Worry causes unwanted and unnecessary stress. This can have a severe impact on our life. At one point, the worry and pressure in my life built up in such a significant way that I had to be hospitalized for over a week. I was ultimately released with no diagnosis other than stress. Life is a rollercoaster ride of feelings, emotions, and situations to juggle. How you deal with them determines the quality of your life.

Find a mantra that resonates with you daily. A mantra is a statement of intention. When I first began meditation, mine was "I am calm." When I recognized I was going down the path of negative self-talk, began to feel fearful or found myself starting to worry, I would repeat: "I am calm." Breathing deeply as I repeated this mantra, I felt myself begin to let go of negativity, worry, and fear. I held onto this mantra for six months until it was ingrained in me. Being calm is now an automatic response for my mind, and my new mantra is "I am joyful."

Worry has never changed the outcome. I gave away many years of happiness to worry. ~ Julie Rizzo

7

SMILE AND
BE HAPPY

1

*"The happiness of your life depends
on the quality of your thoughts."
~ Marcus Aurelius*

Everyone will encounter sadness, frustration, or disappointment at some point in life. We will all experience these feelings. But here is the question: how long do you remain here? Remember, happiness is a choice. Take a minute to recognize and acknowledge how you feel and then choose to move past it. Don't allow situations or people define you– you are in control. Don't let the actions of others impact your happiness!

Think about something that made you smile or laugh. Relive that moment in your mind. What were your thoughts, how did you feel, and what was your reaction? What was it that made you smile and laugh? How do you feel thinking back on that moment? Do you feel happy?

I will share a memory of mine that always makes me smile. Where I live, we have a lock system at the end of our canal, which lifts boats from the canal into the Manatee River. It was mid-February, and we had recently purchased a boat. We had to get a key card and take a class on how to operate the lift. As Joe, our instructor arrived, my husband, John, secured the boat to the dock. We all walked over to the operating system of the lift. My husband has a boating Captain's license, and he is also a firefighter, well-trained in making knots. After 5 minutes, we walked back toward the boat to find it floating in the middle of the canal. The boat hadn't been tied up securely. With no other choice, my husband removed his socks, shoes, and sweatshirt (remember, it is mid-February), jumps in and swims out to the boat in his jeans. Joe, the instructor, looks at me and says, "Well, I have to tell you, this is a first."

John could have been frustrated and upset, and I am sure he was for a moment. But he didn't let the situation define him. The choice he made was to accept it for what it was and not allow it to impact the happiness he felt about his new boat. We still laugh about that today (me much more than John).

Find the humor in life. Life doesn't have to be so serious. Happiness is a choice. If we choose to relax and have happy thoughts, actions, and behaviors, we adopt a joyful life. This doesn't mean we won't feel sadness or have a bad day now and then. When we do, we make a conscious decision to identify how we are feeling and not remain there for too long.

SITUATION & RESPONSE:

You are supposed to go out to dinner with a friend to celebrate your birthday. As you walk up to the restaurant, your friend calls to say something has come up, and they aren't going to make it. Write down your thoughts.

_____
_____
_____
_____
_____
_____

Look at your response above. Is there a more positive way to think? What does that look like? What habits need to shift? Write down your thoughts.

_____
_____
_____
_____
_____
_____

Full workbook is available for download at:
https://findingfulfillmentwithin.com/workbook.html

Disappointment. Sadness. Feelings of being second best. Regret. Frustration. Possibly anger if they have done this before.

These are normal feelings and emotions. But you have control of how long you choose to feel them. In the past, I would have dwelled on these emotions for days, possibly weeks. Now I acknowledge them, put them into a bubble, and let them float up into the sky where they pop. When I visualize them popping in the air, I stop thinking about them. I make a conscious decision to move forward in happiness.

The short-term happiness felt when you purchase a new car can be great, but you must also seek pleasure from non-material sources. Materialistic things only provide short-term happiness. Listening to the birds sing, walking on a beach at sunset, or listening to a baby's pure laughter are "things" that bring us happiness without a price tag.

Helping others brings a deep sense of connection, along with happiness, joy, and pleasure. Have you done something for someone without any expectation because you knew it would make a difference? If you have never done this, or haven't done this recently, make it a point to do it soon. What you get in return is so much more than what you give.

Be happy with who you are, what you have, and who you desire to be. Don't ever wish to be someone else, want for things that others have, or pretend to be someone you aren't. Happiness is living your life right now, making it the best you can with where you are today. Continue moving toward where you want to be. Put a smile on your face and move forward with happiness in your heart.

*"Be happy with what you have.
Be excited about what you want."
~ Alan Cohen*

2

NURTURING OUR BODIES

8 NUTRITION

"Good nutrition creates health in all areas of our existence. All parts are interconnected." ~ T. Colin Campbell

Whole, nutritious, healthy foods and the water we provide for our bodies can be compared to the positive self-talk we give our minds. Whole foods offer our bodies the nutrients needed to fuel them. The water we drink helps carry those nutrients to our cells. The relationship we have with food and water is just as meaningful as our relationship with our minds.

With all the diets out there, how do you know which one is best for you? Would you believe me if I told you it isn't about the diet you choose? It is about the quality and quantity of the foods you eat. It is essential to take a moment to look at what you feed your body. If you find you eat more processed foods than whole foods, you may want to consider making a change. Several benefits come with making this change. But first, you need to determine why you want to make this change.

What is your "WHY"?

Feeling better. More energy. Weight loss. Reducing stress in the body. Consuming fewer chemicals.
Better digestion. Reduce current medicines being taken (with your physician's involvement). Better looking
skin. Improve overall health.

PUT IT IN WRITING:

What is your "WHY?" Close your eyes and imagine your future-self, 30 days from now, accomplishing healthier eating habits. Write down how you feel. What would your future-self tell your present-self about this moment?

_____

_____

_____

_____

_____

_____

Full workbook is available for download at:
https://findingfulfillmentwithin.com/workbook.html

I did not realize how the food I chose to eat affected me the way it did until I went through a twelve-week nutritional course and participated in a cleanse. I saw how my body reacted when I made these changes. I replaced pre-packaged foods with whole foods and removed all products containing gluten or dairy. I added healthy fats to each meal and evaluated what my plate looked like each time I ate. I ensured that I had a high-quality protein, a dense nutrient-packed vegetable or grain, a green vegetable, and high-quality fat.

This experiment lasted seven days. I eliminated coffee and alcohol. I also made a conscious effort to drink more water. It was difficult in the beginning but so worth it in the end. The headaches from the coffee and sugar withdrawal made me want to give up, but I was determined to see how my body would adjust with these changes. I didn't feel better until around day three when the headache started to subside. I felt better than I had in a very long time when I reached day seven.

I ate foods that fueled my body during these seven days. Instead of a bowl of cereal for breakfast, I ate steel-cut oats with blueberries, blackberries, or strawberries. Instead of a protein bar for lunch, I ate a salad loaded with vegetables in all the colors of the rainbow with grilled chicken. For dinner, instead of a frozen pizza, I enjoyed salmon with brown rice and green beans.

I felt healthier and had more energy, good digestion, and less inflammation. Overall, I felt better. So, I continued this smarter way of eating because I felt better, right? Not exactly. I had a few more lessons to learn. After the seventh day, I felt like I was missing out on "good" food so I proceeded to eat half of a large pizza. I was miserable. As I lay awake that night, I realized I had to make a lifestyle change.

As I thought about making this transformation, I acknowledged I had been eating "good" food during the experiment. I felt fantastic, and I was happy with the foods I consumed. I knew that if I wanted to make this lifestyle change, it didn't have to be all or nothing. I would allow myself to have a cup of coffee, a glass of wine, and, yes, a slice of pizza. Telling myself I couldn't have certain things made me want them more, and when I gave into that want, it was devastating.

What you eat and drink plays a significant role in shaping how you feel and think. Your body gets the fuel it needs when you eat whole foods instead of foods high in preservatives. Whole foods give you the energy your body needs through the day. My relationship with food in the past had not been about fueling my body. It was about

2

indulgence, eating whatever felt good at the time. My thoughts about food had to change before I could change my eating habits.

Throughout this section, we will look at ways I was able to make these changes. I will share with you what I learned about nutrition through this journey. As I altered my diet, not only did I feel healthier throughout my body, my mind was also clear. I felt a sense of fulfillment as I worked on both my mind and body together.

"Take care of your body. It's the only place you have to live." ~ Jim Rohn

9

EMOTIONAL EATING

"The foods we eat impact our wellbeing, not just on a cellular level—how we feel, how much energy we have, how strong we are, how capable we can be." ~ Dr. Axe

Do you have triggers that set off emotional eating? I can say, without a doubt, I certainly did. Triggers for emotional eating can come from stress at work, problems in relationships, financial hardship, or health issues. I turned to food as a comfort when trying to deal with the stressors of life. Food also served as a distraction to avoid dealing with tough situations.

Additionally, I found myself turning to food for comfort when I was bored. There were times when I didn't realize I was using food to fill this need until I had already quickly and impulsively consumed it. Only then did I see what I had done. When I learned to pause and understand why I was doing this, it allowed me to choose differently.

How do you break the habit of emotional eating? One way is to keep a food diary. Before you eat, write down what you plan to eat, how much you plan to eat, and the emotion associated with why you are eating. By writing this down <u>before</u> you eat, it identifies patterns and makes the connection between your mood and food. It also allows you to pause to see if your hunger is a physical hunger or an emotional one and provides an opportunity to make a change if needed.

Work on ways to reduce your stress. We will look at mindfulness later in the book and work through means of managing and reducing stress. Take away foods that lead to temptation. If these foods are not easily accessible, you won't eat them. Have healthy snacks like fruits, vegetables, or nuts on hand, so if you need a snack, you have a healthy option.

PUT IT IN WRITING:

How do you break the habit of emotional eating? Take a few minutes to evaluate your routine around emotional eating. What is one small habit change you can make when you find yourself leaning toward emotional eating? Write this down, and commit to making this change in the next seven days.

Full workbook is available for download at:

https://findingfulfillmentwithin.com/workbook.html

If you have a setback, forgive yourself. Do not beat yourself up over it. Recognize the stumbling block, try to learn from it, and think of ways to avoid it. Do not become so focused on the setback that you overlook all of the positive changes you have made up to this point. Each moment, every day is an opportunity for a new beginning. Focus on moving forward.

If you find that you continue to struggle with emotional eating, consider seeking the help of a therapist or other licensed professional. They can help you understand your emotional eating and assist you with ways to work through them. They can also determine if you have an eating disorder and recommend the appropriate help.

2

10 EATING MORE WHOLE FOODS

Let's talk about the difference between processed foods and whole foods. Processed foods are convenient, pre-packaged, easy, and long shelf life foods. Processed foods equate to high amounts of hidden sodium, fats, and sugar. Processed foods go through various processing levels where additional sugar, calories, additives, and chemical preservatives are added.

Whole foods are as close to their natural forms as possible, free from additives, chemicals, and other artificial substances. They are naturally nutrient-dense foods full of minerals, vitamins, fiber, and different levels of macronutrients. Your body can easily absorb the naturally occurring nutrients in these foods, so they are better for your health. In addition to the benefits these foods provide our bodies, less processing, pesticides, and by-products make these foods better for the environment. As you decrease the amount of processed foods in your diet and replace them with whole foods, your body becomes fueled with the nutrients it needs.

Significant, lasting lifestyle changes do not happen overnight. Making small changes each week leads to lasting change over time. The first step is to examine what you currently keep in your pantry. Take a boxed item from your pantry, such as a cereal box, and read the ingredient list on the label. Do you know what all those ingredients are?

Most likely, you can't pronounce some of them. Fewer ingredients indicate less processing, and more ingredients typically indicate more processing.

Let's look at some ways to replace processed foods with whole foods. Take a frozen dinner, for example. Like we discussed, it's easy and convenient. You have a complete meal with an entrée, vegetable, and a starch. You also typically have added sugars, fats, sodium, and preservatives. What if instead, you created your own? Grill some chicken or buy a rotisserie chicken, steam some green beans, roast some potatoes, and put in a freezer-safe container.

Replace boxed pasta with zucchini noodles, potato chips with carrot chips and hummus, dry cereal with yogurt, fresh berries, and granola. Choose a healthy oil like flax, avocado, or olive oil in place of butter. Instead of fried chicken, choose grilled chicken. Make a fresh salad that includes mixed greens with added vegetables, olives, a healthy protein, avocado, and oil and vinegar instead of a protein bar. Your small, gradual changes lead to substantial results over time. Everything does not need to be changed at once.

PUT IT IN WRITING:

What is your goal to reduce processed foods in your diet? Take a few minutes to evaluate some changes you can make to add more whole foods to your diet. Write this down, and commit to making this change in the next seven days.

_____

_____

_____

_____

_____

_____

2

Full workbook is available for download at:
https://findingfulfillmentwithin.com/workbook.html

As we go through each area of nutrition, I will suggest some goals along the way. If you are ready to change your dietary habits, these will give you some ideas to begin implementing these changes. Each little step you take makes a difference. Doing one thing better today than you did yesterday is a step in the right direction. Keep reminding yourself, it doesn't all have to change today, and it doesn't have to be all or nothing. Enjoy your journey.

What you eat and drink impacts how you feel and think. ~ Julie Rizzo

11 WATER, WATER, AND MORE WATER

Drinking water and staying hydrated daily helps our bodies in numerous ways. It helps balance our blood sugar by increasing our energy and decreasing our cravings. Water carries nutrients to our cells and helps our bodies flush out toxins and waste. It helps support healthy kidneys and provides the needed moisture for our eyes, nose, mouth, and skin. It reduces inflammation and lubricates our joints. It also helps prevent muscles from cramping and slows down the signs of aging.

When examining all the benefits associated with drinking water, you may want to ask yourself if you are drinking enough daily. There are several theories of how much water we should be drinking daily. A good rule of thumb is to drink half your body weight (converting pounds to ounces). If your body weight is 150, you would want to get a minimum of 75 ounces of water per day. Keep in mind that sweating expels water from your body, so if you are working out strenuously or are outside in hot, humid weather, you should increase your water intake.

Look at ways to increase your daily water consumption. Try measuring out your water in the morning, so you don't have to keep track of the number of cups you drink. Schedule water breaks throughout the day–set an alarm to remind yourself to drink more water. Make drinking water fun and delicious; add slices of fruit or mint leaves. Drink your water from a beautiful glass. Heat some water and squeeze the fresh lemon juice into it. Not only is this delicious, but it also helps digestion and flushes out toxins in the liver. This is an excellent practice first thing in the morning when you wake up. Look at investing in a water filter. It improves the taste and smell of water.

PUT IT IN WRITING:

What is your goal regarding water? Take a few minutes and evaluate your daily water intake. Should you be drinking more water? What are some ways to accomplish this? Write this down, and commit to making this change in the next seven days.

Full workbook is available for download at:
https://findingfulfillmentwithin.com/workbook.html

12 PICKING HEALTHY PROTEINS

2

Eating the right amount of protein helps balance blood sugar by slowing down the digestion process. When the proper amount of protein is consumed, it slows down the absorption of the carbohydrate-based foods consumed with the protein. Too much or too little protein can cause your body to crave sugar. Exploring how different amounts and sources of protein work for your unique body is helpful. Everyone's body is different, so what works for someone else may not necessarily work for you.

An excellent way to determine which is optimal for you is to track the type of protein you eat, the time you eat it, and how you feel afterwards. Mindfully switch the type of proteins you consume and the time in which you eat them over the course of three days. If you eat three meals per day, you would select an animal protein for one meal, a plant protein for another, and no protein at all for your third meal. Over the course of the three days, rearrange this sequence so that you consume different protein types at different times of day, while carefully monitoring your mood and energy levels. Pay particular attention to how you feel one to two hours after eating. Look at which protein gives you more energy, keeps you feeling satisfied longer, and generally works to fit your body's needs. This exercise will help you determine which protein, at which meal, is most beneficial to your body.

PUT IT IN WRITING:

What is your goal regarding protein? Take a few minutes to plan your 3 Day Protein Challenge. What will this look like for you? Looking at your schedule for the next seven days, when can you commit to completing this challenge? Write this down and commit to doing this in the next seven days.

_____

_____

_____

_____

_____

_____

3 DAY PROTEIN CHALLENGE

Each of the 3 days, for breakfast, lunch, and dinner, choose an animal protein for one meal, a plant protein for one meal, and then eliminate the protein completely from one meal. Switch the timing of these proteins for your meals over the next 2 days. Track how you feel one hour after eating at each meal and then two hours after eating. You can determine how your body responds when you eat animal protein versus plant protein versus no protein and at which time of the day each is the most beneficial. Which one gives you more energy, keeps you feeling satisfied longer, and works best for your body.

Day	Meal	Protein Type	Foods Eaten With Protein	Energy	Mood
1	Breakfast				
1	Lunch				
1	Dinner				

2

Day 1 Thoughts:

_____

_____

_____

_____

Day	Meal	Protein Type	Foods Eaten With Protein	Energy	Mood
2	Breakfast				
2	Lunch				
2	Dinner				

Day 2 Thoughts:

_____

_____

_____

_____

Day	Meal	Protein Type	Foods Eaten With Protein	Energy	Mood
3	Breakfast				
3	Lunch				
3	Dinner				

2

Day 3 Thoughts:

_____

_____

_____

_____

PUT IT IN WRITING:

Evaluate all three days together from the protein challenge.
What provides the highest energy/best mood for you?

_____

_____

_____

_____

_____

_____

Full workbook is available for download at:
https://findingfulfillmentwithin.com/workbook.html

13

ADDING HEALTHY FATS

Knowing the different types of fats and the foods associated with them will allow you to make the healthiest choices. Healthy fats are essential to every meal. Adding these kinds of fats to each meal leaves us feeling more satisfied after eating. When we don't include fats, it can lead us to over-indulge and leave us wanting more.

Avoid trans fats as much as possible. Many of these are man-made and are added to foods for flavor and to extend their shelf life. Most cakes, cookies, and crackers contain trans fats. These products incorporate shortening, which contains partially hydrogenated vegetable oil. Many types of chips (potato, corn, tortilla, etc.) contain trans fats, as do fried foods. This type of fat increases "bad" cholesterol and lowers "good" cholesterol.

Although better than trans fats, saturated fats are still not considered to be healthy. Some proteins high in saturated fat include beef, pork, bacon, lamb, processed meat, some cold cuts, and breakfast sausages. Cheeses, cream, butter, and certain plant-based oils like coconut, palm kernel, and palm oils also have high saturated fat. Monitor how much of these are in your meals.

Unsaturated fats are the healthiest of all and should be included in daily meals. There are two different types of unsaturated fats: monounsaturated and polyunsaturated.

Although they only differ slightly, including both types in appropriate proportion helps support the immune, cardiovascular, and central nervous systems.

Monounsaturated fats contain only one double bond in their molecular structure. These fats are found in several healthy foods, including avocados, almonds, cashews, pecans, and peanuts. Olive, canola, sesame, and peanut oils along with pumpkin and sesame seeds are all great examples of monounsaturated fats. Replacing unhealthy fats with monounsaturated fat can have a cholesterol-lowering effect.

Polyunsaturated fats are broken into two types of fatty acids: Omega-3 and Omega-6. These fats are essential in our diet because our bodies cannot produce them. Sources of Omega 3 fatty acids include fatty fish like salmon, mackerel, sardines, anchovies, and herring. Omega-6 fats are found in safflower and sunflower oils, walnuts, sunflower seeds, hemp, and tofu.

PUT IT IN WRITING:

What are some ways you can incorporate healthy fats in your diet? Take a minute to evaluate what types of fats you currently include in your meals. Do you have a healthy fat with each meal? Look at some ways to include healthy fats in each meal. Write it down, and commit to doing this over the next seven days.

_____

_____

_____

_____

_____

_____

14

FRUITS, VEGETABLES, GRAINS, AND LEGUMES

Fruits, vegetables, whole grains, and legumes provide numerous health benefits. These foods provide fiber in our diets. They help you maintain a healthy weight and lower your risk of diabetes and heart disease.

The body does not digest fiber. It passes relatively intact through your stomach, small intestine, large intestine, and colon, then out of our bodies. Fiber breaks down into two classifications; soluble, which dissolves in water, and insoluble, which does not.

Soluble fiber helps lower blood cholesterol and glucose levels and is found in beans, oats, apples, citrus fruits, and carrots. Insoluble fiber promotes the movement of materials through your digestive system. Insoluble fiber benefits individuals who struggle with irregular stools or constipation. This type of fiber can be found in cauliflower, green beans, potatoes, nuts, beans, and whole wheat flour.

Good sources of fiber include whole-grain products, fruits, vegetables, beans, peas, other legumes, nuts, and seeds. Keep in mind, the refined or processed versions of these foods, such as canned fruits and vegetables, white bread and pasta, and non-whole grain cereals are lower in fiber. Refined grains are produced through a process which removes the grain's outer coating, lowering its fiber content. This is why choosing whole foods is key.

Here are some tips to fit more fiber into your diet. Choose a high-fiber cereal (*whole grain*, *bran*, or *fiber* in the name) with five or more grams of fiber per serving. Switch to whole grains; look for bread that lists whole wheat, wheat flour, or another whole grain as the first ingredient. Add peas, lentils, and beans to soups and salads. Make snacks count; raw vegetables and fresh fruits are good choices. A handful of nuts is also a healthy choice for snacking, but keep in mind that nuts are high in calories, so limit portions accordingly.

PUT IT IN WRITING:

What is your goal regarding fiber? Take a minute to evaluate how you are currently getting fiber in your diet. Would it be beneficial to add more fiber? Look at some high-fiber foods you can include in meals. Write these down, and commit to adding these over the next seven days.

_____

_____

_____

_____

_____

_____

Full workbook is available for download at:
https://findingfulfillmentwithin.com/workbook.html

If you are just beginning to add high-fiber foods, add them slowly. Adding too much fiber too quickly can cause abdominal bloating and cramping, along with intestinal gas. Increase fiber gradually over a few weeks. It is also important to wash or peel all fruits and vegetables before eating, especially those that are not organic and have been sprayed with pesticides. Make sure you are drinking plenty of water as you increase fiber. Water, along with the fiber, will help to improve your digestive system.

2

3

NURTURING OUR SPIRIT

We have reviewed how to cultivate our minds by removing negative self-talk and working on positive habit changes. We have also evaluated how to take care of our bodies through proper nutrition. Now, we will look at how we can nurture our spirits through self-care.

For many years, I did not make self-care a priority in my life. This was an area I put on my list for "if I have time." I didn't make "me" important enough. I allowed almost everything to take a front seat to self-care.

Nurturing our spirits through self-care allows us to experience moments of calm, relaxation, serenity, tranquility, and peace. Self-care increases happiness, peace, and joy while reducing stress, anxiety, and depression. Your body and mind come into harmony when you make self-care a priority in your life.

"It is important to take time for yourself and find clarity. The most important relationship is the one you have with yourself." ~ Diane Von Furstenberg

15   BEING MINDFUL

"Almost everything will work again if you unplug it for a few minutes. Including you."
~ Lindsey O'Connor

The Oxford dictionary defines mindfulness as "a mental state achieved by focusing one's awareness on the present moment, while calmly acknowledging and accepting one's feelings, thoughts, and bodily sensations; used as a therapeutic technique."

Clearing our minds and permitting ourselves to practice mindfulness allows us to be in the present moment without judgment. There are many ways to practice mindfulness; meditation, deep breathing, journaling, and living with gratitude. It is essential to plan for this each day. Life gets busy, and we often allow our lives to be run by the busyness. When we take a moment to stop and practice mindfulness, it slows down the pace and brings us back to the current moment.

There are several benefits associated with practicing mindfulness. You allow yourself to be fully aware of both your emotional and physical state of mind. Seeking mindfulness reduces stress. Cortisol, which helps the body deal with stressful situations, is released when the body feels it needs to be protected. If too much cortisol is released, it can cause serious problems such as weight gain, digestion issues, and high blood pressure. The overproduction of cortisol can also adversely affect sleep patterns, contribute to muscle weakness, and cause memory and concentration problems.

Meditation, along with a deep breathing practice, brought me out of the downward, spiraling freefall I found myself in. This practice was extremely uncomfortable at first. In the beginning, I felt silly lying still, listening to someone guide me through deep breathing, while focusing on different parts of my body. At the time, I didn't understand how valuable this practice was going to become in my life.

As I continued this practice, the calmness and peace I felt cannot be put into words. My mind and body were in harmony together. I still begin each day with this practice. Before starting my journey, I had to monitor my blood pressure because it had become so high. I allowed my life to control me instead of taking control of my life.

Guided meditation is a great way to introduce this practice into your life. This type of meditation provides a focal point for your mind. A guided body scan leads you through the practice, drawing focus to each part of your body. You connect fully to your physical-self. This opens the mind, providing a sensory experience which allows the body to relax. There are many free meditation apps available. Try several of them, and when you find one that resonates with you, purchase it for full access. It will be money well spent. Insight Timer is my favorite app for meditation.

Another healthy way to practice meditation is by visualizing your future-self. Picture yourself living your best life. See it in your mind as if your goals have already been achieved. You will feel accomplished when you visualize yourself having successfully obtained whatever it is you want. Turn on some peaceful music and set a timer. Take a moment, and clear your mind. Give thanks for where you are on your journey and get excited when you visualize where you are going.

Putting thoughts down on paper brings mindfulness to your life. Journaling in a pretty book or typing out your thoughts on a computer is a great way to release feelings. I call this a "mind dump." Get all of the thoughts out of your mind. This is a freeing experience, and one that creates calmness and peacefulness in the mind. Writing this book helped me help myself. Make the time to experience what this feels like for you. If it is helpful, schedule it! Schedule time in your day to make mindfulness happen.

Take time to practice gratitude. When you recognize where you currently are on your journey, and what you are thankful for, it helps remind you of all you have to be grateful for. We all face challenges in life. But we also have numerous things to be thankful for. Take a minute now to just sit and think about all the positive aspects of your life.

PUT IT IN WRITING:

What is your goal for mindfulness? Take a minute to evaluate where you currently are with this practice. What are some ways you can make more time for mindfulness in your life? Write these down, and commit to adding one of these over the next seven days.

3

Full workbook is available for download at:
https://findingfulfillmentwithin.com/workbook.html

16 GET MOVING

"The body benefits from movement, and the mind benefits from stillness."
~ Sakyong Mipham

Movement is one of the most important things you can do daily, and yet many of us, myself included, sometimes consider it optional. Any type of movement we give our bodies is free medicine. Even the smallest movements can improve your health and change your outlook. It doesn't matter how young or old you are or what your current endurance level is; everyone benefits from movement.

Sometimes finding the energy and making the time are the biggest challenges we face when it comes to including movement in our day. If you can't commit to 30 minutes, break it up into three 10-minute sessions. Remember, small changes over time can yield tremendous results.

Movement helps control blood sugar and weight, lowers blood pressure and cholesterol, and promotes heart health. Daily activity increases bone strength, improves sleep patterns, and reduces stress. These benefits alone should encourage us to commit to

3

movement daily.

Making exercise fun is the key to making it part of our day. When you enjoy the type of activity you choose, it becomes more of something you "want" to do and less of something you "have" to do. There are many choices when looking at ways to add movement to your day. I have listed out some of these below. Try several of them, find which ones bring you the most enjoyment, and integrate them throughout your week.

Start with a short 10-minute walk around your neighborhood. Not only will it add movement to your day, but it can also give you a sharper, calmer mindset. The experience of being outside, listening to the birds, watching the squirrels, and feeling the wind on your face provides so much more than just movement. Start with 10-minutes in the beginning and increase it by 5 minutes over the next few weeks, gradually bringing it up to 30 minutes.

Yoga is a beautiful way to add movement to your days. It combines exercise that supports both the body and the mind. It incorporates breathing combined with movement, which helps reduce stress and improves flexibility, endurance, strength, and balance in the body. Yoga shifts your perception and mindset. Don't be intimidated by the poses—you don't need to be experienced to practice yoga. There are numerous videos on the internet to get you started in your own home. This practice added more than just movement for me. Through yoga I learned a deeper level of meditation and found a greater sense of peace.

Do you belong to a fitness center? Are you currently exercising on a treadmill, climbing the elliptical, or riding a stationary bike? Do they offer group exercise classes at your fitness center? Be open to trying something new. Don't feel intimidated by others in class. Everyone in the class had their own first class. In fact, in my experience, most people will encourage you if you let them know you are trying the class for the first time. You may find that you really enjoy this class, and if not this one, try a different one.

Do you already have some small weights at home? Is watching television part of your daily routine? Grab the weights and do some sets while you watch your favorite show. If you search the internet for light weights exercises, you will find a few that will work for you. Start with a low pound weight and gradually begin increasing a little at a time as you feel comfortable. Even just some light stretching exercises using weights is a great way to include movement in your day.

PUT IT IN WRITING:

What is your goal for movement? If you don't currently include regular exercise in your life, take a minute to evaluate how to add it. If you do engage in regular activity, assess how much enjoyment it brings you. Are there different types of movement you can try? Write these down, and commit to adding a new type of movement over the next seven days.

Full workbook is available for download at:
https://findingfulfillmentwithin.com/workbook.html

3

The biggest takeaway here is to include some type of movement daily. If you sit at a desk all day, be sure to make time to move. Set a silent alarm to remind you each hour. Make the most of this free medicine. Be sure to include your physician when deciding which type of movement is best for you.

17

SLOWING DOWN THE PACE

"Take a deep breath. Get present in the moment and ask yourself what is important this very second." ~ Gregory McKeown

How often do you find yourself going from one thing to the next? Do you find yourself thinking, "I don't even know where my day went"? We need to remind ourselves that life is a journey. It is not a race to see who can get through it the quickest. When we get to the end, we want to know we have lived it to the fullest. Take time to enjoy the life you have been given and live it with fulfillment.

By slowing down the pace, we become present. We take opportunities to enjoy special moments. We learn to savor those moments by taking pictures in our minds, so we can recall them later. We learn that we don't always need to be doing something. Find ways to become present, and slow down when you realize you are rushing to the next thing.

When you find yourself in a rush, ask yourself why? Is there something you could have done differently that would have allowed you more time? Would starting 10 minutes sooner have given you the time to enjoy the moment more? Be conscious of the small changes you can make to slow down the pace.

Multitasking increases stress and splits your focus between the tasks you are trying to complete. You can't slow down when you are trying to do multiple things at once. Focus on one thing at a time, and be present with that one thing. Disconnect from technology. Put the phone down, and be in the moment.

When we add unwanted stress in our lives, the hormone cortisol steadily floods into our body. The release of cortisol is a positive reaction if we are in danger—it serves to protect us. But when we continuously put ourselves in a position where our body feels the need to be protected (especially when there's no real threat), the resulting build up of cortisol will harm the body.

Take a serious look at your life when you feel like you are going a hundred miles an hour. Eat slower, so your body will digest a little easier. Drive slower, and savor the ride a little more. Slow down your life, and delight in the journey. Enjoy each moment to the fullest. You can't get them back once they go by. Cherish your time!

"We will be more successful in all our endeavors if we can let go of the habit of running all the time, and take little pauses to relax and re-center ourselves, and we'll also have a lot more joy in living."
~ Thich Nhat Hanh

PUT IT IN WRITING:

How can you slow down the pace? Take a minute and evaluate how quickly you are moving through life. Can you find some ways to slow down and enjoy present moments more? Write these down, and commit to doing one of these over the next seven days.

_____

_____

_____

_____

_____

_____

Full workbook is available for download at:
https://findingfulfillmentwithin.com/workbook.html

3

18

LEARNING HOW TO RELAX

"Your mind will answer most questions if you learn to relax and wait for the answer."
~ William S. Burroughs

Relaxation, for many of us, is difficult. We become so busy working, rushing the kids to after school activities, planning and making dinner, or taking care of personal things, like laundry and grocery shopping. You get the idea. We often allow the busyness of our lives to devour our time.

We all need to take time to relax. I remember times when I had an extra ten or fifteen minutes, but instead of relaxing, I found a way to fill the time. I felt that if I didn't use that time for something productive, I had wasted the "extra" time. I wish I had known then what I know now. Relaxation is something I must consciously practice. With dedication, it has become more natural for me to relax, but this did not come easily. There are often times when I tell myself that it is okay to "check-out" for ten minutes. We must allow our mind and body to relax. Think about your phone. When the battery runs low, it switches to power-save mode. It is drained and needs to be recharged. It's no different for us. We need time to rest and recharge our batteries in order to operate at our best.

Relaxation helps manage stress and pain in the body and mind. Most relaxation techniques are quite affordable. Many of them are free. It takes less than two minutes to de-stress the body. The more relaxed you are throughout the day, the more energy you will have. Relaxation, just like movement, helps improve your outlook and perception.

An easy way to turn off the sympathetic response in the body, otherwise known as the "fight-or-flight" response, is by practicing conscious breathing. This activates the parasympathetic nervous system, which we could call the "feel and heal" response. When you focus on your breathing, your mind concentrates on pulling in new energy with each inhale and pushing out stale energy on every exhale. The body's response is to relax as you do this. The more often you practice this, the quicker the body will respond.

A useful trick for deep breathing is to make the exhale twice as long as the inhale. Breathe in for a count of 4 seconds, hold for a count of 4 seconds, and exhale for a count of 8 seconds. Try this now. See how your body begins to relax, and your mind begins to clear. Remember, it takes less than two minutes for the body to relax.

Once the body is relaxed, a quick body scan can help ensure all parts of your body have participated in the relaxation process. When you find an area where you are holding tension, take a moment to breathe into that area. Starting on the left side, begin at the foot and mentally scan up the leg to the hip. Do the same for the right leg. Come up through the torso, down the left arm, and back up, then the same for the right arm. Move up through your neck, ending on the crown of your head.

Another technique is to actively use your senses. Close your eyes, and focus on what you hear. Try to find five different sounds. Once you recognize five sounds, concentrate on a place in your mind which brings you a feeling of peace and calm. Imagine you are there and envision what you see, what you smell, and what you hear.

Permit yourself to relax. You will find that when you take the time to practice relaxation, your days become more fulfilled, and you find more happiness, peace, and joy in your life. Take two minutes and allow your body to embrace relaxation.

PUT IT IN WRITING:

What role does relaxation play in your life? Evaluate where you are for a minute. How can you add relaxation practices to your days? Write these down, and commit to two minutes every day over the next seven days.

_____

_____

_____

_____

_____

_____

Full workbook is available for download at:
https://findingfulfillmentwithin.com/workbook.html

3

*"If you're always racing to the next moment,
what happens to the one you're in?"
~ Nanette Mathews*

19

LIFE BALANCE

"Balance is the key to everything. What we do, think, say, eat, feel, they all require awareness, and through this awareness, we can grow." ~ Koi Fresco

What does it mean to have life balance? Life balance occurs when you focus your time equally on the most important areas in your life. It is when you feel calm and grounded daily. Life balance is finding fulfillment each day within your mind, body, and spirit; enjoying all aspects of your life: work, family, social life, and self-care.

So, how do you achieve life balance? It doesn't just happen; it requires a plan. Acknowledge your current situation. Where do you find yourself today? Do you find one area of your life takes a front seat more than another? When most people evaluate their lives, adjustments are typically needed to get the balance they want.

If you are doing something that isn't adding value to your life, stop doing it. You will be amazed at how much time you might spend aimlessly scrolling through social media

3

sites or mindlessly watching television. When I stopped giving my time to these two things, I gave myself an extra two hours per day: fourteen hours each week!

Let go of the time you spend focusing on negativity. Minimize any negative influences in your life. Instead, surround yourself with enthusiastic people, positive habits, and a "can-do" mindset. It is essential to recognize when one part of your life should be put on pause so that another part can begin. This is how you will achieve balance in your life.

Changing the structure of our daily lives helps create the balance we need. Eliminating things that waste our time gives us more time for things that provide balance to our lives. When we identify what those things are that create balance in our lives, we find more clarity and fulfillment.

To determine what balance looks like for you, take a moment to consider these ten areas: Career, Creativity, Finances, Health, Joy, Movement, Relationships, Self-Care, Sleep, and Social Life. What would you need to do to create balance in this list? How many hours of sleep do you need? How many hours does your job require? What does it look like to spend time with your family? What about time with your friends? How much time do you need for self-care? This might include working out, preparing healthy meals, and meditation. What about hobbies or recreational activities?

Determining what gives us balance brings us closer to achieving it. Take time monthly to evaluate where you are. Doing this provides an opportunity to make adjustments along the way. As life shifts, the balance will shift. By revisiting this monthly, you will see where changes are needed.

PUT IT IN WRITING:

How does your life balance look? Take these ten areas: Career, Creativity, Finances, Health, Joy, Movement, Relationships, Self-Care, Sleep, and Social Life, and evaluate each one by rating them between 1 and 10. 1-3 indicates the area doesn't receive a lot of focus, 4-6 indicates it gets a fair amount of attention, and 7-10 indicates it gets too much emphasis. Look at ways to pull from those areas between 7-10 and push to those areas between 1-3. Write down ways to shift focus, and commit to doing this over the next seven days.

Full workbook is available for download at:
https://findingfulfillmentwithin.com/workbook.html

3

20 CONTENTMENT

"To be content doesn't mean you don't desire more, it means you're thankful for what you have and patient for what's to come." ~ Tony Gaskins

Being content does not mean that we can't choose to make changes in our lives. Instead, it means we accept where we are in our journey and continue to work toward where we want to be. It is being thankful for the life we currently have while being excited about the one we are creating. Contentment is taking each moment in our lives and accepting it for what it is and trusting that you are supposed to be right where you find yourself at this moment.

Sitting back, relaxing, and being grateful for where you find yourself brings forth feelings of contentment. When you let yourself fully appreciate all you have achieved, you create a sense of fulfillment and peace. Simplifying your life helps reduce unnecessary stress. By making things easy and learning to not take everything so seriously, you improve your outlook on life. The inner peace we feel is fueled by the simplicity we create.

3

Worldly things will not fill us with contentment. They may make us happy in the short term, but many times, they do not sustain happiness in the long run. Being content means having our needs met; not all of our wants fulfilled.

Find your purpose and practice contentment. Take time to honor yourself and those around you. You will find more happiness, joy, and peace when you appreciate where you are. Accept that you are right where you're supposed to be while you continue to make changes that will lead you to where you want to be.

PUT IT IN WRITING:

What does contentment look like in your life? Take a moment to honor yourself for where you are right now. Look at ways you can simplify your life and add more contentment. Write these down, and commit to doing these over the next seven days.

Full workbook is available for download at:
https://findingfulfillmentwithin.com/workbook.html

21

FINDING FULLFILLMENT

Finding fulfillment is a life-long journey. Learn not to take life so seriously; have fun, and be happy. Take time to play, rest, and, most of all, take care of you. Choose to live your life with happiness, peace, and joy. ~ Julie Rizzo

Finding fulfillment in life is what we all want, right? Yet we make it so much more complicated than it needs to be. Sometimes we find ourselves so wrapped up in thinking about the past or future, we miss living in the present day. Don't let life pass you by. In my past, many days just came and went. I did not stop to take the time to appreciate a single moment during the day.

Cherish as many moments as possible throughout your day. Take an opportunity to watch the sun rising or setting, the birds flying in the sky, the leaves rustling in the wind, the waves lapping on the water, the snow glowing on the mountain top. Find pleasure in small moments and cherish them. Pause and take a picture in your mind. Go back to this vision when you feel stuck and unhappy. Free yourself, and live presently each day.

Do something daily that brings you closer to **Happiness**, **Peace**, and **Joy**. Stop worrying about the past; you cannot change any of it. Time has moved on, and so should you. Don't worry about the future. Worry doesn't change the outcome; it robs us of our present moments. If there is something you want to change in your life and can change it, just do it and stop over-thinking it.

Find little things that bring joy to your day. Take the time and appreciate them. Live in gratitude, and treasure where you're at today. Make the small changes, and create those positive outcomes. Live your life to the fullest every day. You never know what tomorrow may bring. Thoroughly enjoy the journey along the way, finding fulfillment overflowing with happiness, peace, and joy. You deserve it.

PUT IT IN WRITING:

What does your journey to fulfillment look like? Take some time to evaluate what small changes you can make that will bring you closer to happiness, peace, and joy. Write them down, and commit to yourself, right now, to do one thing over the next seven days to bring you closer to living your life with fulfillment.

_____

_____

_____

_____

_____

_____

Full workbook is available for download at:
https://findingfulfillmentwithin.com/workbook.html

"Health is a state of complete harmony of the body, mind, and spirit. When one is free from physical disabilities and mental distractions, the gates of the soul open." ~ B.K.S. Iyengar

3

4

SETTING GOALS AND TRACKING OUTCOMES

22 SETTING GOALS

*"This one step—choosing a goal and
sticking to it—changes everything."
~ Scott Reed*

You have already begun making small changes in your life. Each of these small shifts bring you closer to the life you want to live. Are you ready to continue the journey? If not now, when? Recently something resonated deep within you to pick up this book. Now is the time. Take a deep breath, let it out, and say to yourself, "I've got this!"

You may have started your journey as you read through this book by completing the "Put it in writing" sections. The entire workbook is available to you at the following link: https://findingfulfillmentwithin.com/workbook.html. If you decided to first read through the book, take an opportunity now to go through the exercises. These will help you determine what your top goal will be over the next 60 days. I will guide you through simple goal-setting exercises and ways to commit to making small changes over the next 60 days. These small changes will lead you to find your fulfillment.

4

We have reflected on ways to change your mindset by making a conscious decision to look at positivity instead of negativity. As you continue to focus on positive areas in your life, you will find yourself experiencing more happiness.

We have also looked at how nutrition is a critical factor in how we feel and think. How the foods we feed our bodies have a direct impact on our energy, digestion, and overall well-being. Additionally, we reviewed how drinking water nourishes our bodies just like the foods we eat. By committing to make small changes in your nutrition, you will continue to give your body the fuel it needs to experience optimal health.

Finally, we tapped into our spiritual selves. When we allow the mind to be quiet and the body to be active, along with nurturing our bodies and minds, the results are life-changing. If you are genuinely ready to commit to changing habits through implementing small changes over time, anything is possible.

Setting goals and tracking outcomes is the best way to stay the course. If we set a goal but never revisit it or evaluate how much of that goal we accomplish, we may never meet that goal. Many people have great intentions by setting goals at the beginning of each year. Yet many do not return to evaluate and modify them. This is one of the reasons that the goals most people set are seldom fulfilled.

Think about one area you want to focus on over the next 60 days. It could be related to any of the topics we reviewed in this book, or perhaps it relates to something else you want to accomplish. Remember, it does not have to be all or nothing and does not need to be achieved in one day. Small steps over time will produce long and lasting results. This gives your mind, body, and spirit time to adjust and gradually accept the changes.

As I take you through setting goals, you will answer a series of questions related to the goal you just identified. Take the time to think through your answers to these questions. Write down your answers. This process supports your decision for change. It will allow you to revisit what you felt when you set your goal and enable you to revisit your thoughts.

60 DAY GOAL

This is a short-term goal. You know this is within your reach over a short period of time. You know by making small changes to this area in your life, you will have more fulfillment. Write down this goal. You are going to commit to doing this over the next 60 days.

_____

_____

_____

_____

_____

_____

Full workbook is available for download at:
https://findingfulfillmentwithin.com/workbook.html

Now that you have written down your goal, you need to know your "WHY" for wanting this. Defining your "WHY" provides clarity and purpose surrounding your goal. What are some of the reasons you want this? Give this some thought, and, when you are ready, write down your "WHY" in detail. This is an important step. Don't skip over it.

Once you have determined your "WHY," look at how reaching this goal would make a difference in your life. By achieving this goal, what changes would you see in your life? This could be anything from feelings and emotions to stability and finances. How would these changes impact your life?

What will it feel like once you have met this goal? What do you notice about this feeling? Picture your future-self having accomplished this goal. How does this feel?

4

What do you need to let go of to get this? Are there things you are holding onto that will prevent you from accomplishing this goal? What is holding you back?

What is one action step you can commit to taking in the coming week to begin working toward this goal? What do you need to take this action step? When will you start? Make it a point to pick a specific day for this coming week in which you will put your plan into place and begin working toward it.

What could get in your way of reaching this goal? Life happens, so think about the obstacles that might derail you from reaching your goal. Be prepared for them, and expect them. Have a plan for any obstacles you can foresee.

What support will you need? Who can help you accomplish this goal? Share your goal with a loved one, friend, or coach. Ask for the support you feel you will need. By sharing your goal and asking for help, these individuals can encourage and cheer you on along your journey.

Who else might benefit when you reach this goal? Are there other people in your life that will be positively impacted when you achieve this goal? What about people not currently in your life? How could successful completion of your goal benefit others?

Congratulations on setting your 60-day goal, digging in deep, and answering the questions surrounding it. You can also do this for other areas in your life where you are ready to see changes, even if more than 60 days are needed. You can do this for a 6-month goal, a 1-year goal, or even a 5-year goal. The key for achieving goals is making follow-up appointments with yourself to evaluate them.

60 DAY GOAL SETTING

My 60 Day Goal – What do I want to accomplish in the next 60 days?

_____

_____

_____

Why do I want to accomplish this?

_____

_____

_____

How will this make a difference in my life?

_____

_____

_____

How will I feel when I accomplish this?

_____

_____

_____

4

60 DAY GOAL SETTING

What do I need to let go of to accomplish this?

_____

_____

_____

What action step will I commit to in next 7 days to begin?
(Be specific in your answer with the date you will take this action step.)

_____

_____

_____

What might get in my way of accomplishing this?

_____

_____

_____

What support will I need to accomplish this?

_____

_____

_____

60 DAY GOAL SETTING

Who else might benefit when I accomplish this?

_____

_____

_____

Additional Thoughts

_____

_____

_____

_____

_____

_____

_____

_____

_____

_____

_____

_____

_____

4

6 MONTH GOAL SETTING

My 6 Month Goal – What do I want to accomplish in the next 6 months?

_____

_____

_____

Why do I want to accomplish this?

_____

_____

_____

How will this make a difference in my life?

_____

_____

_____

How will I feel when I accomplish this?

_____

_____

_____

6 MONTH GOAL SETTING

What do I need to let go of to accomplish this?

_____

_____

_____

What action step will I commit to in next 7 days to begin?
(Be specific in your answer with the date you will take this action step.)

_____

_____

_____

What might get in my way of accomplishing this?

_____

_____

_____

What support will I need to accomplish this?

_____

_____

_____

4

6 MONTH GOAL SETTING

Who else might benefit when I accomplish this?

_____

_____

_____

Additional Thoughts

_____

_____

_____

_____

_____

_____

_____

_____

_____

_____

_____

_____

1 YEAR GOAL SETTING

My 1 Year Goal – What do I want to accomplish over the next year?

_____

_____

_____

Why do I want to accomplish this?

_____

_____

_____

How will this make a difference in my life?

_____

_____

_____

How will I feel when I accomplish this?

_____

_____

_____

4

1 YEAR GOAL SETTING

What do I need to let go of to accomplish this?

_____

_____

_____

What action step will I commit to in next 7 days to begin?
(Be specific in your answer with the date you will take this action step.)

_____

_____

_____

What might get in my way of accomplishing this?

_____

_____

_____

What support will I need to accomplish this?

_____

_____

_____

1 YEAR GOAL SETTING

Who else might benefit when I accomplish this?

_____

_____

_____

Additional Thoughts

_____

_____

_____

_____

_____

_____

_____

_____

_____

_____

_____

4

23

TRACKING OUTCOMES

"What gets measured, gets managed." ~ Peter Drunker

Evaluation is where the change truly happens. This is where you take time to consider what is going right, what you might need to modify, what obstacles are getting in your way, and where you are in reaching the desired outcome. This process allows for adjustments. If you don't schedule these appointments with yourself and put them in your calendar with reminders, chances are, you will not come back to evaluate them. Tracking outcomes brings you back consistently to why you wanted this and why it was necessary.

Tracking outcomes in writing allows you to see what is working and leads you closer to reaching your goal. Praise yourself as you track these outcomes. You are accomplishing great things! Tracking also helps you to identify areas where you might benefit from making small tweaks to your plan.

In this chapter, there is a "Tracking Outcomes" section for each goal. Take time now to look at a calendar and schedule the dates when you will review each goal. Block off time for yourself now, and set a reminder for these dates on your calendar, just like you

4

would for any other appointment.

Keep this important appointment with yourself. Give yourself the time needed to evaluate where you are with each goal, what you are doing right, and where you might need to adjust. Write it all down. Give yourself kudos for what you have accomplished so far. Review the areas where you can still improve your plan. Do not beat yourself up about pieces you haven't met. Simply recognize them, and permit yourself to make the changes needed to accomplish them.

For the 60-day goal, schedule time every week over the next eight weeks to review your goal. For a 6-month goal, you will want to schedule time every three weeks. For a one-year goal, every six weeks. Commit to this! It will be life-changing.

As you reach one goal, set the next one.. Every day is an opportunity to live your best life. By setting goals and tracking outcomes, we become the person we want to be. The small changes we make daily help us achieve the life we want to live. Make yourself a priority and commit to reaching your goals.

I find that revisiting sections of this book each time I sit down to track my outcomes is especially beneficial. It reminds me of why I am doing this and validates my purpose. Use this book as a tool. When you find yourself sliding back into old habits, revisit a relevant section of this book to refocus you toward your path to success.

Full workbook is available for download at:
https://findingfulfillmentwithin.com/workbook.html

60 DAY GOAL TRACKING OUTCOMES

Week 1 - 60 Day Goal Review Date _____

Evaluate % Completed _____

What is going well? What can I modify? How do I feel?
What is my next action step?

_____

_____

_____

Week 2 - 60 Day Goal Review Date _____

Evaluate % Completed _____

What is going well? What can I modify? How do I feel?
What is my next action step?

_____

_____

_____

Week 3 - 60 Day Goal Review Date _____

Evaluate % Completed _____

What is going well? What can I modify? How do I feel?
What is my next action step?

_____

_____

_____

4

60 DAY GOAL TRACKING OUTCOMES

Week 4 - 60 Day Goal Review Date _____

Evaluate % Completed _____

**What is going well? What can I modify? How do I feel?
What is my next action step?**

_____

_____

_____

Week 5 - 60 Day Goal Review Date _____

Evaluate % Completed _____

**What is going well? What can I modify? How do I feel?
What is my next action step?**

_____

_____

_____

Week 6 - 60 Day Goal Review Date _____

Evaluate % Completed _____

**What is going well? What can I modify? How do I feel?
What is my next action step?**

_____

_____

_____

60 DAY GOAL TRACKING OUTCOMES

Week 7 - 60 Day Goal Review Date _____

Evaluate % Completed _____

**What is going well? What can I modify? How do I feel?
What is my next action step?**

_____

_____

_____

Week 8 - 60 Day Goal Review Date _____

Evaluate % Completed _____

**What is going well? What can I modify? How do I feel?
What is my next action step?**

_____

_____

_____

Additional Thoughts

_____

_____

_____

_____

4

6 MONTH GOAL TRACKING OUTCOMES

1st 6 Month Goal Review Date _____

Evaluate % Completed _____

**What is going well? What can I modify? How do I feel?
What is my next action step?**

_____

_____

_____

2nd 6 Month Goal Review Date _____

Evaluate % Completed _____

**What is going well? What can I modify? How do I feel?
What is my next action step?**

_____

_____

_____

3rd 6 Month Goal Review Date _____

Evaluate % Completed _____

**What is going well? What can I modify? How do I feel?
What is my next action step?**

_____

_____

_____

6 MONTH GOAL TRACKING OUTCOMES

4th 6 Month Goal Review Date _____

Evaluate % Completed _____

**What is going well? What can I modify? How do I feel?
What is my next action step?**

_____

_____

_____

5th 6 Month Goal Review Date _____

Evaluate % Completed _____

**What is going well? What can I modify? How do I feel?
What is my next action step?**

_____

_____

_____

6th 6 Month Goal Review Date _____

Evaluate % Completed _____

**What is going well? What can I modify? How do I feel?
What is my next action step?**

_____

_____

_____

4

6 MONTH GOAL TRACKING OUTCOMES

7th 6 Month Goal Review Date _____

Evaluate % Completed _____

**What is going well? What can I modify? How do I feel?
What is my next action step?**

_____

_____

_____

8th 6 Month Goal Review Date _____

Evaluate % Completed _____

**What is going well? What can I modify? How do I feel?
What is my next action step?**

_____

_____

_____

Additional Thoughts

_____

_____

_____

_____

_____

1 YEAR GOAL TRACKING OUTCOMES

1st One Year Goal Review Date _____

Evaluate % Completed _____

What is going well? What can I modify? How do I feel?
What is my next action step?

_____

_____

_____

2nd One Year Goal Review Date _____

Evaluate % Completed _____

What is going well? What can I modify? How do I feel?
What is my next action step?

_____

_____

_____

3rd One Year Goal Review Date _____

Evaluate % Completed _____

What is going well? What can I modify? How do I feel?
What is my next action step?

_____

_____

_____

4

1 YEAR GOAL TRACKING OUTCOMES

4th One Year Goal Review Date _____

Evaluate % Completed _____

**What is going well? What can I modify? How do I feel?
What is my next action step?**

_____

_____

_____

5th One Year Goal Review Date _____

Evaluate % Completed _____

**What is going well? What can I modify? How do I feel?
What is my next action step?**

_____

_____

_____

6th One Year Goal Review Date _____

Evaluate % Completed _____

**What is going well? What can I modify? How do I feel?
What is my next action step?**

_____

_____

_____

1 YEAR GOAL TRACKING OUTCOMES

7th One Year Goal Review Date _____

Evaluate % Completed _____

**What is going well? What can I modify? How do I feel?
What is my next action step?**

_____

_____

_____

8th One Year Goal Review Date _____

Evaluate % Completed _____

**What is going well? What can I modify? How do I feel?
What is my next action step?**

_____

_____

_____

Additional Thoughts

_____

_____

_____

_____

_____

4

DAILY REFLECTIONS

Reflect on each day at the end of the day and recall the special moments you cherished and appreciated!

What opportunity did I take today to be with nature? How did it make me feel?

_____

_____

_____

What is something that brought me happiness, peace, or joy today and had me smiling?

_____

_____

_____

How did I remain in the present moment today?

_____

_____

_____

DAILY REFLECTIONS

What were my takeaway moments from today?

_____

_____

_____

Additional Thoughts

_____

_____

_____

_____

_____

_____

_____

_____

_____

_____

4

CONCLUSION

FINDING YOUR FULFILLMENT WITHIN

"Vulnerability is not winning or losing; it's having the courage to show up and be seen when we have no control over the outcome. Vulnerability is not weakness; it's our greatest measure of courage." ~ Brené Brown

This quote has resonated with me for many years. She also said, "When we deny our stories, they define us. When we own our stories, we get to write the ending." That is what I have chosen to do – own my story and write the ending. Through this journey, I have learned that my happiness, peace, and joy will never be found outside of myself; it can only be found within.

This book was never something I planned to share with the world. I started writing to put into words what I needed to do to find my happiness, peace, and joy. A month after I started writing, I decided to investigate other ways to help myself. I found a life coaching and nutrition certification course. I was torn between signing up for the course and hiring a life coach myself. I was also on the fence about returning to school. So, after a lot of debating, I decided to sign up for the course. I didn't anticipate it would change my life.

Not only did it change my life, it also changed the lives of the people closest to me. I discovered ways to change my mindset and have a positive outlook on my life. I realized what I was eating had an enormous impact on all areas of my life. I found closure and peace from losing my mom over twenty years ago. Ultimately, I discovered I could help others find their way to a more fulfilling life.

This was the beginning of Finding Fulfillment Within. A company I created to coach others to nurture their minds, bodies, and spirits, and guide them to find true fulfillment in their lives. Happiness, peace, and joy are attainable. Sometimes it just requires someone showing us how to find it.

I never realized how powerful having a coach could be. Through the course, we worked with other students and we also worked with success coaches. The work I was able to do with others throughout the course was incredible. The encouragement, support, and accountability I had with my success coach were priceless. I encourage everyone to seek this level of support.

That is why at Finding Fulfillment Within, we offer a Free 30-Minute Transformational Discovery Break-Through Session. During this session, you will discover what you want, what is holding you back, and put the right system in place to have inevitable success in achieving it.

I would love to hear from you. Please go to our website, www.findingfulfillmentwithin.com and leave a comment. We would love your feedback on the book and how you are using parts of it on your life's journey. I can also be reached directly through email at julie@findingfulfillmentwithin.com.

If working with a coach is something you have never experienced, or if you have worked with a coach in the past and want to experience it in a way you never have before, log onto our website and schedule your free 30-minute session today. You have nothing to lose and everything to gain. Thank you for reading this book. I hope it was as life-changing for you to read as it was for me to write. Here's to living your best life and finding fulfillment within!

www.findingfulfillmentwithin.com

ACKNOWLEDGMENTS

To my husband, John. You will always be my best friend and confidant. Thank you for believing in me and helping me through the times I didn't believe in myself. I would not be the person I am today without you. I can't put into words how your much your humor, kindness, support, and love over these past 30 years have meant to me. I love you, babe – forever and always!

To my beautiful daughter, Rachel. I am so proud to be your mom. Always know you can accomplish anything you put your mind to. Hard work and dedication will always pay off in the end. Stay true to yourself in everything you do and keep happiness, peace, and joy at the forefront of your life. I love you buddy!

To my Dad. I am so grateful to have you as a dad. Thank you for showing me how to create a solid foundation in which to continue building on. I cherish the time we spend together, and I am blessed to be your daughter. I love you daddy!

To my closest friends—Jenn, Rhonda, Julie, Tim & Cindy, Danny & Colleen, Kirk & Kim, Bobby & Candace—thank you for always being there for both me and John. Thank you for coming along on this journey with me and being my biggest cheerleaders. Your edits, feedback, and encouragement along the way, and the memories we created together, have been priceless.

To Mark Hickman and Shari Bench—It was my honor to work for you both during my 25 year career in the Healthcare Industry. The lessons learned during these years helped form me into the person I am today. Thank you for trusting me and allowing me to grow with you both.

To Two Penny Publishing—Thank you for all your hard work in helping my vision become a reality. Your editors, designers, and entire staff have been an absolute pleasure to work with. Thank you to Tom and Jodi for encouraging me, supporting me, and helping me become a best seller.

To all the people that have passed through my life—teachers, friends, coworkers, authors, pastors, coaches, and all the people I met just in passing—thank you for having an impact on my life. You have all inspired me to be the person I am today. You have taught me kindness, compassion, forgiveness, contentment, and most of all love.

To all the people that read this book—I hope this book has helped you discover how to let go of the things that have been holding you back and you have found ways to live your absolute best life ever with happiness, peace, and joy, leading you to finding your fulfillment within.